PAINT-BY-NUMBERS WORLD

Paint-By-Numbers World

POEMS

Cassondra Windwalker

Paint-By-Numbers World

Copyright © 2026 Cassondra Windwalker
First Edition

Paperback ISBN: 9781965412442

Cover art and design by Jacob Arms

Published by Broken Tribe Press
William K. Lawrence, Editor In Chief
Lawrence Landing Company
Raleigh, North Carolina 27609
USA, North America
www.brokentribepress.com

Broken Tribe Press is a proud member of:

Independent Book Publishers Association
 and

Community of Literary Magazines and Presses

Praise for *Paint-By-Numbers World*

"If a poetry book can be a page turner, *Paint by Numbers World* is it. Every poem in Cassondra's contemplative, biting, fly-on-the-wall-of-the-world collection is like a chapter that takes your breath away and beckons you to read just one more. The raw, often concise language precisely captures and reveals uncomfortable truths that range from the political to the personal—sometimes delivered with a tenderness that seems to ache, other times with a hard, cold stare. Written with the clarity and compassion that is born out of lived experiences, these are magical meditations, hushed shouts, and active reminders that beauty and its dark underbelly are twin souls that live within and around us all."

—Michelle Meyer, author of *The Trouble with Being a Childless Only Child*

"Poetry that speaks to me ideally comprises three elements: a feel for language so that it can be used in the most impactful way possible (language to me is always a form of music, and your poetry sings to me); language that creates strong visual images and even tactual ones--placing the reader inside the physicality of the poem; and language that doesn't reveal all its layers in one reading but continues to peel back, each time the poem is read, to draw the reader in more deeply--and the reader can sense those layers in the first reading. This collection encompassed all those for me."

— Tracy Wise, author of *Madame Sorel's Lodger*

For Duffy and Ryska

CONTENTS

First World, Second World, Third World

We all share the same blood, the same bones, the same rotting skin, but we look for mock differences to justify our mistreatment of each other. Likewise, the lot of women around the world differs radically from the lot of men, whether it is the countless missing women of North America or the mothers and wives and daughters of Madagascar, who often bear the brunt of poverty in their wombs and in their vaginas. We all need the same water to survive, and we will all drown in the same sea.

Madagascar

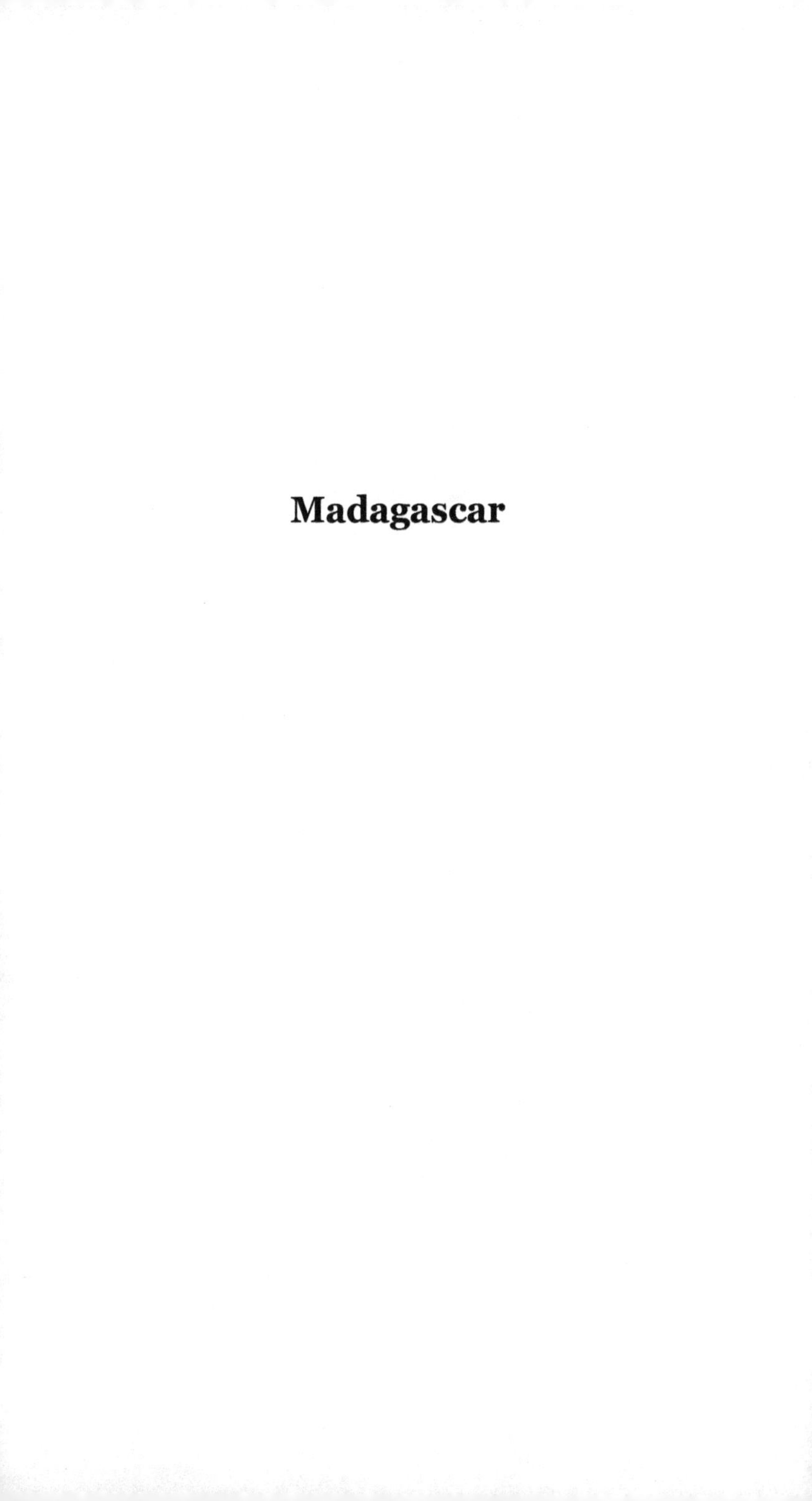

hat in hand

I have learned to live between hinges,
inside suitcases, books, laptops:
houses always seem to belong
to someone else, their colors and absences of colors
demarcating my space, their walls
and doorways always thresholds to rooms
in which I am a guest, an interloper –

perhaps one day I will find a porch,
a windowseat, an attic garret whose soft wood
swallows whole all my wild colors,
all my words, but till then I lie
my head safe between these covers
and send my mannikin to sleep in a stranger's bed.

Punk Love Mahajanga

of a thousand women in a hundred yards,
she is the one I see –
perhaps it is her shoulders, tossed back high
like epaulets – perhaps it is her rolling,
flat-footed gait that makes every stride
a claim of conquest – perhaps it is the turn
of her head that bids even the sun

to wait

wait

on her command before it dares to gilt
her unvarnished skin, but my mind conjures
a queen where a tired woman walks
in denim jeans and a white t-shirt that proclaims
Punk Love across her back – I see
something flash in the black eyes,
I see sun-parched cracks in the thick yellow paste
she has smeared on her face,
and I think

I think

I hope

I am right, I hope the t-shirt is right,
I hope she is a she that rises and conquers
and then sets free.

life at sunset

I am retreating into my own sublimity

no longer clinging to the jagged edges
of what was never mine to hold,
breaking free of definition
as comprehension unravels – I move
from becoming into being,
surrendering all my hoarded pennies
so I may bathe my skin in gold.

how long this road

unevenly the wooden wheels of the zebu cart
clamber along the road below me, out of sight
beyond the palm trees, an arrhythmic beat
beneath this dawn-song of birds and beetles
and rustling fronds: I wonder how far
he will go today {they are always *he* here,
on the zebu carts, or driving the beasts
with sticks down the road} -when he will return,
what he will have done, if tomorrow,
the clattering feet of the wooden wheels
will carry him farther, or if his road
will only ever be the distance
of a day in the zebu-cart.

the rebellion of color

even the flowers here are faded,
worn out with the weight of their colors
beneath this sun, but in the streets,
the hues are insistent, brash, splayed
with abandon on sun-baked dirt,
rotten tarps, and staggering shacks:

women deck themselves in sunrises
and sunsets, and the people paint, paint, paint,
stamping impossible colors, impossible names,
impossible claims on every surface
where my blind eyes would imagine
the greed of a too-hot sun and too-cool men
have baked all possibility out.

Are They Orphans, I Asked

They are not all orphans,
but they are all in the streets,
she tells me, with a look that says
you know what I am saying,
and I nod, clinging to the edges
of her meaning but never really seeing
the inside – on the inside,
the skin of children is stamped with ariary
and euros and dollars, traded simply
as ready orifices for haughty French
and sweaty American and entitled Malagas men:

They are not all orphans,
but they are all in the streets.

water-girl

she trudges toward the gate-house,
dark skin ghosted with white chalk
from the steady pick-pick-picking
of men who squat in the sun
and turn big rocks into little rocks,
her bare soles stained red
from the silty earth she navigates, sure-footed:

she could chip rock, too,
but she is more valuable carrying the empty water jug
toward men in uniforms who watch her approach
with greasy eyes – they are dressed up
like guards in shirts bought with the money
of American do-gooders, but the garb
of protection does not assuage the hunger
of the fossa – they will bite and tear

they will eat up her eyes
so she cannot see herself,
and then she will carry water back
to the men pick-pick-picking,
she will sit under the palm tree
until it is time to be eaten again.

red earth

heat sifts quietly into my cells,
dislodging memories of another red land
but the same sun – I am unwilling
to listen to the wind as he shifts against me,
prodding me with his flat, sullen hands
that like the shade, only pretend at relief:

I have heard their words before,
I am not fooled by their new clothes,
whether raising palm trees or cottonwoods,
red dirt is the color of thirst,
the color of exile, the color of a ransom
that will not be paid.

stratification

it is music in her hands,
the lyrical susurrance of rice on woven grass
as she tosses it again and again,
stray grains sparkling in the sun
like lost diamonds as they fall into the sand:

she readies charcoal on the brazier,
stands flat-faced in its shimmering gaze
as the heat that already chokes me
billows around her – she cooks the rice,
spoons it onto our plates, and before
she can duck away, I see hunger
pretending at hope in her eyes,
but that is foolishness.

her sister scrapes her portion,
her children's portion,
into the plates of American guests,
and sends her outside.

wretchedly I scoop gritty rice into my mouth,
wonder what they would say if I told them
I too have been mother to fatherless children.
there is rice in my mouth,
but I taste only dirt.

brothers-in-arms

I saw at least a hundred children
today, beetling hard-nosed and blind-eyed
between stalls and cattle, buses and mopeds,
but no mothers – or else mothers are indistinguishable
on these streets from vendors of fruits
or vegetables or other goods as brightly jacketed
in color and dirt: these two boys
I cannot forget, though how they are
more memorable than any other
is as mysterious to me as my own purpose here:

nine and six, I think, perhaps ten and seven,
tiny dark bird-bones strung together
with fierce sinew and will, each struggling
steadfastly forward under his burden –
the older, a full sack of rice whose fifty pounds
must have nearly exceeded his own weight,
the younger, equally staggered by half a bag –

a moment only, and we had passed them.
still, I see the younger boy's eyes fixed
so yearningly on his brother's back,
the elder's fixed on finding a path through,
and I keep hoping and hoping
they made it, when I know there is
no it.

to dream like dogs

the beach here is empty,
probably because les grands hotels
keep the common riff-raff away
but maybe too because the waters
washing up on white sand are all red mud –

on the horizon I spy blue water
but here it looks more like a plague,
and I have no desire to coat my sweaty skin
with this miry sludge as well:

I retreat to shade and watch two fishers
struggle past, their tiny rusted bark powered
only by their two oars as it fights the sea,
and two of Madagascar's singular pups,
one white and one black, come to sleep
curled at my feet in the sand while I scribble,

and I vow, as I always vow,
and am always oathbreaker,
to attain the verity and contentment of dogs.

dead man's ticket

the ocean is a railroad where it meets the shore:
its tracks, like all men's tracks, are laid
in blood, they cross lands on which
they have no claim, they offer only passage,
never safety, but still the sound of that engine
rushing into the station, the cry of that whistle
to go ever farther out and farther on
is surely more than the most sedate and rational
of minds can resist: here, though,
on this island, the ocean is so much farther
than the shore – murky red waters girdle
the sand – even the seagulls do not loot these tides;
in fact, no birds at all venture
beyond the trees. I wonder how far here
a man must swim to catch a train,
if he even hears the whistle as it passes.

a bit of advice

we must enjoy, he says,
a bright grin splitting his face
beneath his lazy eye, and I think
of the baobab trees growing tall
and immense and solitary in a small forest
on a small island on a small planet,
only they two for company in all the universe.

the baobab are not frightened by their singularity,
they feel no urgency to reproduce,
no inclination to protect a future they do not see,
no need to defend the years past
in which they grew: they are content
to enjoy the sun warming their leaves,
the rains soaking their roots,
the strange occasional caresses of human hands
on their trunks, the meandering steps of ants
and birds and beetles and lemurs.

we must enjoy, he says,
and we must stand, I think, like the baobab,
and this is enough.

the wife

he wears a white polo shirt,
catches a bus to work where there is
air conditioning and toilets and clean well water:

she stays home, horizoned by thin metal walls
and a straw roof, where darkness brings
no respite from the choking heat,
where dirty water comes dear in a yellow plastic jug.

she has one baby in her arms,
another she must keep from the open door,
and three children she teaches to read.

she is coconut:
patient and still, but break her open,
and she is meat and milk,
food and drink,
strength and hope.

the cyclone and the shore

storm gasps and sighs as she falls
astride her lover – come ashore, he whispers,
and she does, settling herself across
the mighty thighs that buck and toss
beneath her – inhale and exhale,
her breaths quicken, winds rise
and abate, palms flatten and cower
then stand trembling to full height
until her pleasure crests again –

this is no onslaught, no relentless offense,
but the wild and savage culmination
of too long an absence, too wide a distance
that even these two know
can only be abridged these few hours:

so they make the most of it,
breaking the bedstead, tearing the sheets,
till she is forced back into servitude
across the sullen grasses and must make
the long travel across oceans again,
before his kiss brings ripe all her rain.

slower or swifter

I attend on snails today,
bring my breaths into resonance
with the dip and sway, dip and sway,
of their questing antennae,
set my heartbeat to the metronome
of one crushed blade of grass
and then another

perhaps I have gained a year
this way, perhaps twelve:
I raise my eyes, starstruck by a sun
I had forgotten in the weighing
and sifting of life by grains of dirt
rather than the spinning of worlds –
it seems to me this day
has a name, or had a name –
perhaps I do too,
but for now, I am attendant only on snails.

I turn my gaze back to the traveler
and find him already gone, outpacing me.

two babies and a bowl

We are driving past.

I see the hesitation, the uncertainty
in a man's eyes as he looks down on them –
twin infant boys, sitting, crawling,
perhaps walking age, propped up
in the fine dirt of the street teeming
with taxis, buses, feet, and bikes,
maybe five feet from the safety of the sidewalk.

We are driving past, but my eyes
seize on the beggar's bowl before them,
a woven basket with a chunk of rock to keep
the money safe – must keep the money safe,
at least – the hand-blocked placard in a language
I can't read. One boy tips over,
catches himself with a tiny hand
on his brother's knee – the merchant
watches them still, arrested in his course
with the cart of bread that he must push
along to the stalls, along to the market –
I see reluctance to leave them in his eyes,
only his, as everyone else bustles by,

and then we have driven past.

Thank God for the Lutherans

Lutheran Hospital, the sign proclaims –
at least I think it does. This is the good hospital,
the good hospital, the good hospital,
I tap out onto my palms as we walk by
patients clutching bags and tubes, leaning
against wooden pillars on the long narrow porch –

a camp hospital room, its twelve beds
festooned with frilly lace mosquito netting
in every pastel shade, stands framed
by open doors and windows – I imagine
the Lutheran ladies picking out pink and blue
sheets to match their tinted white hair, wonder
how they cluck at the costs of the oft-reused
and stained-black urine cups and bedpans.

The patient's wife brought him a bottle of water,
and for now there is no pain, but tomorrow morning
he must leave. No soap or sanitizer in this room.
I stare at the dirty edge of his lovely pink sheet –

*Pass the potatoes, won't you, dear? Oh, they'll be
so grateful, so grateful. Let's sew some
pillowcase dresses next* – and I think about the blade
that cut his skin, the hands that repaired the cut.

This is the good hospital.

she has no road

he does not see the sunrise
in her eyes as he cycles past,
an obelisk of charcoal teetering
on the bicycle seat behind him – all he sees
is the road, a shifting viper
who coils and strikes and coils again:

buses screech past, porters swinging
one-armed from the bumpers,
tuk-tuks and mopeds and three-legged taxis
fight for right-of-way as barefoot children
and basket-laden women squeeze past,
but all he can do is pedal and balance,
pedal and balance,
and trust that the snake will not bite him today,
that the ancestors will reward his offering
of charcoal with rice and send him back
down the road after sunset tonight:

she sits in the dust, heated darkness
pressing warm against her skin
till she sees him cycle past, empty
of charcoal, laden with rice,
and she counts her calendar
by his returns,
swears to herself she never dreams
of a departure of her own.

rhythm of reset

when the rain falls, the snails appear,
heedless of the sun's course,
and begin their tireless march:
they do not regard stone or wall
or arroyo as a grief – they simply go
up and down and through
until the heat says hide

and they hide

until the rain says come

and they come

I think I will simply wait
for the rain, and then I will
go up and down and through,
till the heat says hide.

bibliography

I want to grow huge and old
and fat like the mountain, songs
carved like rivers into the granite
of my skin, craggy boulders erupting
from my fingers, moss creeping
everywhere the shadows linger,
and bears and birds alike content in my palm:

I want to grow slow and strange
and twisted like the baobab,
hoarding secrets like water and unfurling
a limb or a burl every century or so,
following a path to the sky no-one sees
till I build it, keeping close
all my records and rendering sterile my replicators:

I want to grow dry and cracked
and forgetful as the arroyo,
every flood and drought, each turn
and rush and stop-short remembered
by the desert floor, my body a repository
of steps and stories, stones and currents:
I want to grow.

Alaska

winter blooming

ghosts of summer trees stomp their feet,
shake out their skirts and dance
in the dark fir court of the winter gods,
dance off the snow and the ice and the cold,
dance off the night clinging to their bare limbs,
dance off the stars that fall
and keep falling into their brittle fingers:

I want to dance like a summer ghost
and make winter stand still about me,
but my roots are frozen, locked in the frost,
my bark is caught in the teeth
of the moose, the elk, the caribou,
my stick-fingers snag in the lace
of the sky and snap off, falling like icicles
into the snow:

I want to dance like the dead,
but I am too alive, too dull, too stupid,
for that. I unlace my heavy boots, though,
and walk barefoot in the snow,
pretend my toes are asters, marigolds, and bluebells.

the dead do not answer to old names

what is the name for a frozen sea jelly?

they spangle the beach today,
glistening like dropped stars among chunks
of broken ice and shattered anemones,
suspended in their were and yet new
and entirely other in this so still now:

I think of another wanderer who did not want
to be, who tried so hard to keep her feet
to a regular path, but a cold wicked tide
stole her away too, tossed her up unseen
on some hidden shore where all her motion
has become immobile: her mother calls
out a name, again and again,
but this frozen star on the sand
does not answer, cannot return to sea or sky.

almost beautiful

I watch skinwalkers stride over whitecaps
like fog dancing on ice-bound waves
and almost it is beautiful to watch
them dance, almost I do not smell
the blood rising, almost I pretend
they have become legend when they have only
become bones: in the sand, in the muskeg,
in the mud, in the snow, my feet sink
in the rot of the missing,
I pluck berries that burst with blood
on the tongue, I am pricked and torn,
looking for the flesh that hangs
in shreds, for the bloodied ankles that buried
my sisters as they fought. almost
this place is beautiful,
beautiful like fungus leaping from soft flesh,
like men's mouths agape with hunger.

tracker

oily footsteps mark the streets
till the road all but disappears:
their boots are mired thick
with the blood of the missing,
that swampy soup of blood and bone and soul
from which they never lift their ankles free:

I see their shadows in the fog
behind, before me, I follow their tracks
and fight the wind for their names,
but they are less real than the dead
and more easily hid

still, I do not forget. I read faces
and filthy palms, I count the breaths
too slow for prey, I walk
up and down the muddied streets,
searching for the end. these are not wolves,
after all, merely coyotes,
and I am much more than a rabbit.

moose and me

we breakfast together,
moose-colt and me,
bemused but undeterred
by the windows and walls
making two of our one meal:
he eats black-skinned, gownless
rosebushes, their thorns a thousand
fierce, insistent arms –
I eat coffee and biscuits,
and between us, we resolve
to consume the morning whole:
snow and sun and hopelessness,
the snapping of cameras
and babbling of headline-mourners,
we eat them all,
chew the pith with the thorns,
swallow all the words, words, words
and wait for our bellies
to empty again.

vigil

withered hands hold cardboard signs
against a winter sun, shout affirmations
that frost and freeze and shatter
in the air – they seek a lost sheep,
but she is not lost
she is eaten, she is devoured,
she is torn from her own limbs
and she cannot hear their call

I see the mark of claws in the snow,
I feel the rotten steam of his breath
hanging in the air, and my mouth
is empty of these promises they recount:
I hope they find their sheep,
what poor fleece and hooves remain,
but I seek the eater,
it is his name I repeat in my sleep.

the fisher's wife is a moon

he's trying to get her pregnant
before fishing season, I hear him say,
and I sip my coffee and stare
out the window, into the bay,
think of silver-bellied salmon flashing
through black seas and glacier-green rivers,
many moons whose phases spell out
the seasons of eating and fasting,
and I think of a moon-girl rising
silver-eyed and round-bellied
on the shore of the sea, watching the waves
for a boat that will not come home.

devotion of age

she practices an adoration of decay,
makes relic of barnacles,
builds shrines of bone and shell
and driftwood, crushes sandcastles
like incense and sends them out to sea
on a shouted prayer –

she does not mourn
the many-colored incursions of fungi
and algae, of outcast sea stars and sea jellies:
she glories in the hues seen only
in the twilight shadows, she traces
the lines on her neck and decks them
with leather string and broken carbuncles.

let others fade out, become paper,
become tissue, painted like skin
and shredded in the tide – she will break
her own bones to build a new ship,
she will trade her braids
for moss curtains and lend her hands
to the sea-dragons, her feet to the selkies.

a fixture in the town

he spindles in, knob-kneed
and bloat-bellied, a caricature
of a joke with creases that know how
to look like a smile, with a gleam
in his eyes pretending at a twinkle,
and in the fiddle-faddling and tomfoolery,
I catch the practiced turn
of an expert's hand: harmless,
the grown-ups say, the men say,
but genteel old ladies look away,
eyes sliding, fingers twisting, feet shifting,
and the joke ends with no punchline:

he spindles back out again
with a cheery wave and a chorus of good-byes,
and Jocelle and Nancy and Edith
rush home to stand in steaming showers,
scrub sagging skin and fading freckles,
but the secrets he scrawled on their bones
are writ too deep to wash away.

cemetery leaves

I am talking to the leaves
lying in the ruts of the dirt road

crickets skitter, baby-size, across
the dirt, but I do not regard them:
they have nothing to relay,
nothing they know – fresh-hatched,
they only skitter
frantic, fearful, foolish

but the leaves – or, rather,
the skeletons and spectres
of last autumn's discards, these intrepids
who have clung to the dirt
under heaps of snow
and heaps of ice
and heaps of darkness, unremitting,
unrelinquished, through all the months
of winter and her griefs, her hungers

I am talking to these leaves
and finding out all my bones,
my dried and worn and stretched flesh,
my bloodless veins that still scream
like racing roads under the sun

I am talking to the leaves
as if neither of us were headstones.

commune

trees hunch together in sun-drenched
stillness, waiting without patience
but without recourse for the advent of dark
in this northern summer – a breath huffs
on the other side of the clustered limbs,
heavy feet clatter through dust and rocks,
and softer still, the sound of square teeth
stripping branches of their burdens commences –

we stand together, the moose and I,
separated only by a copse of pine and alder:
in this quiet bide, our two breaths
are the only wind – we see the same night,
smell the same dying clover and prowling bear,
and perhaps we even dread the same winter,
trust in the same resurrection of spring.

song for the unfound

in the upside-down of the up-above,
birdsong condensates in twilight
like the sea under the sun,
melody ascending the midnight stairs
as if the darkness will never come:

for a while it seems the birds are right,
their hopeful trills and drowsy staccatos
keeping stars and other, less noble, nightwalkers
at bay – but the dark will have her way
in the end – she will bundle up
birdsong into baskets and send it back,
she will sew celestial buttons bright
into the fabric of the night and fasten it
securely against the pale flesh of the sun,
she will call out the eaters and the creepers
and let them have their way.

for now, I hope your bones are content
to believe what the birds believe,
that you rest easy in the twilight of in-between,
that you take the flowers of this brief season
as the due of your out-of-due-season grave.
I hope you rise in shining drops of song
and lend some sign of your departure,
that we the left-behind may make meat
of your wretched eater yet.

not-midnight

there is no darkness
but still the night is lightless

it does not rain
but water drips ceaselessly from the leaves

the still air is cloyingly sweet,
a syrupy intoxicant clinging
to my throat and nose and bare skin,
rotten sugar rising from wet flowers
and last year's leaves and the bodies
of the missing we have forgotten to find

the birds sing unsilenced
by the mere measure of hours,
and I imagine it is they who keep
both night and light at bay,
they who make of twilight a curtain
that shuts us in on this side
the window, shuts us in
with the dead and the lost and the waiting

to see if we will open the window
in the end and make a way through

or be ever still in the not-night
and the not-rain, not-listening to the not-truth.

revolt

the ravens are all dead

the salmon choke out
on rocks at the ocean mouth

and the tide has cast off
the tug of the moon

no? no.

it is only one more skull
piled outside the city gates,
only one more feast to fill
the bellies of the fat,
only one more lie told as truth
to wax-filled ears

so I will still pick among the carcasses,
make meat of misery, find food
for fury in the bodies of my brothers,
send sun-lit flames flashing
from ebony wings to the eyes of the blind

I will swim upstream, I will transform
from silent grey to crimson outrage,
I will plant my seed and glory
as its life consumes my own

I will turn to the moon
and say, drive me,
drive me against this sand

together let us mold
a new earth
and alter all these shores.

driftwood

I have not lost time –
my bones keep count,
growing rings like trees,
but time loses me from tide to tide,
cutting me adrift
and snatching up buoys
so that I cannot find a channel home:

I must go the long way round
in the end
to the end
sometide before the end:
some cannier sort could have navigated
more directly, no doubt, but I am all
tangled lines and smudged maps
even when the water is clear

and this water is not clear,
there is sand and salt in my eyes:
so the long way round it is

and I am all rings upon rings,
burls and knots and dying stars
by the time I spy the harbor:

I will not make it, after all,
but still I am glad I knew the open sea.

I Search A Still Thing

I have searched for birds
who set the limbs a-tremble, strained
for the graceful canter of the deer
or the knobby meander of the moose,
I have watched the brush and listened,
fear-stricken, for the heavy gait of the bear,
but this is different.

Today I look for a still thing, a silent thing,
placeholder for a soul long departed.
I dare not call her name – to conjure
affirmation of her absence in this place
that teems with presence is its own horror:

so I creep in dread of my own noise
and seek a stillness, a void, an arrested,
I sift leaves for fingernails, examine
roots and limbs as if they might be bones,
but her still self, her quiet unbecoming
unhappens elsewhere, hidden too well
by a beast unashamed of his own ill-fit skin.

Song for the Apocalypse

evening comes on:
it is August, so perhaps
the midnight sun will be abed
by midnight, and not pace
and peer with pale, bloody eyes
along the seams of our dreams:

evening comes on,
and mushrooms bloom fetid and garish
from the dying body of the earth,
berries flush over-sweet
and everywhere spent petals fall –
I choke on the fragrance

and wait on this night, this dark,
this still, this cooling of the flesh
that has fought so hard.
tears will become frost,
fight and fear become flaccid,
and I – and we – and this awful hour –
will all unbecome at last.

evening comes on,
and the nightingale begins her song.

Death and her Spinning Wheel

this fetid forest pretends at welcome,
as if this lush carpet that swallows my feet
were other than yarn unspooled
by the nimble fingers of the dark spinning-mistress
whose sewing room this is:

I am not lured by her loveliness –
her dank perfume offends my nostrils,
and I count as carcass
each new blooming swath of strange and spectacular
fungi who masquerade as magic:

each flowering mound is only the corpse
of some tree pulled to its death
by the lady's unstitching, and even now
I count in the rustling leaves her eager breaths,
I watch her fingers brush the hanging moss
as if to measure a bolt for her veil,
and I feel her needle pricking at my heels –
she will unwind me yet, but not today.

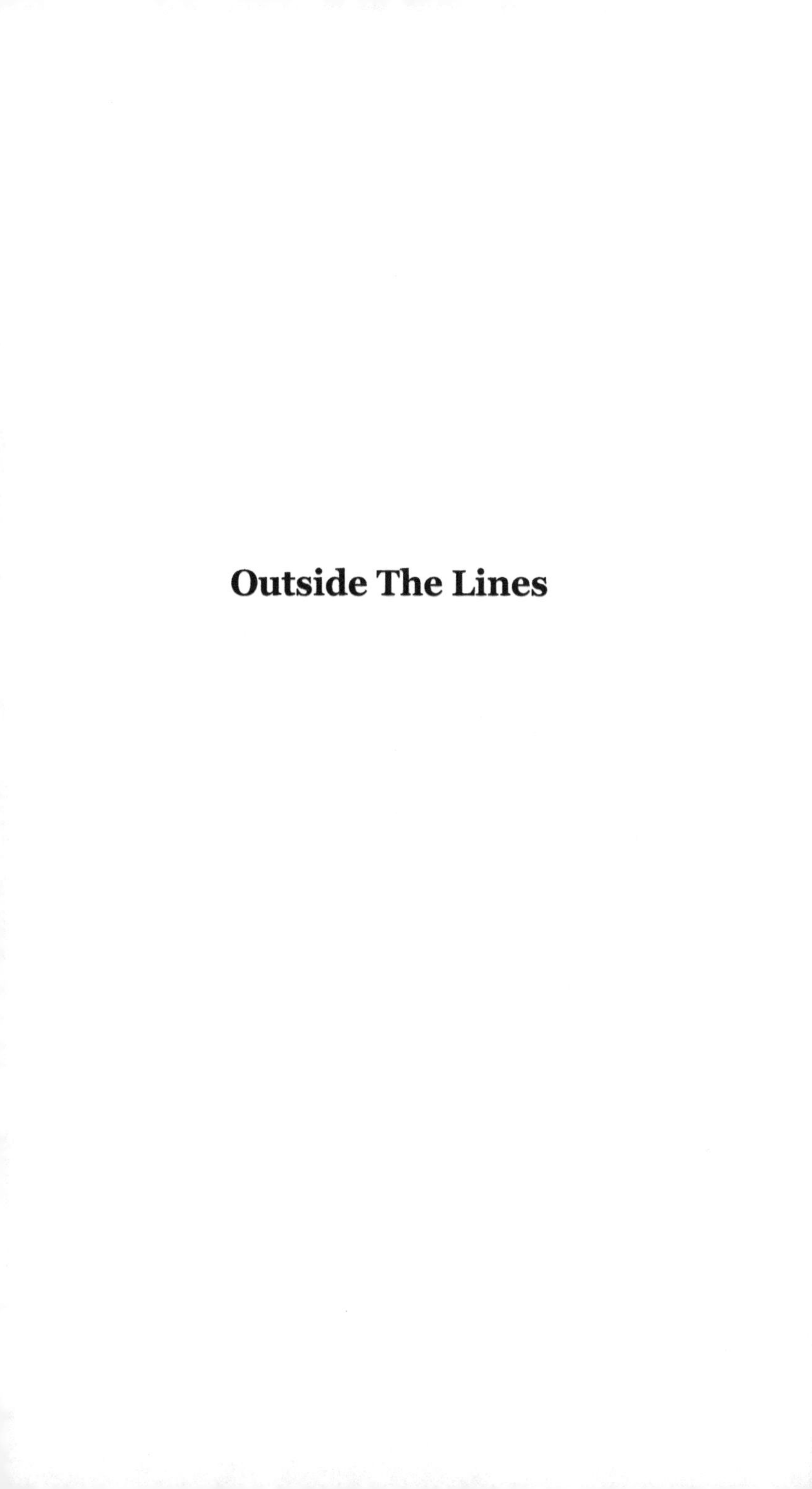

Outside The Lines

Paris is for painters

my mind is Jackson Pollock,
looking for Picasso, who is muttering
to Kahlo about Manet, but my words
are all Matisse, and I am drowning,
drop by drop: the scene, the city, the song,
suffuse me till all my lines are circles.
rifle-strapped policemen at the doors,
the train station, the streets (there are policewomen
in France, too, aren't there?)
tiny paintings lined up on a broad old bridge
over filthy water, colossal stone lions growling
over rotten mattresses, moss-gowned angels sighing
over heaps of trash, everywhere grace and art,
sweat and craft, beauty and discipline,
bending over fury and disdain, graffiti and garbage:

a burned cathedral staggers to her feet,
a crowd pushes against riot shields,
a young woman peers out from her rain-spattered stall
at the Christmas market, wonders anxiously
who will buy her ornaments this year.
Popova. Popova could make sense of this.

separation

no two people ever stand on the same side of a grave.

do you feel the wind blow?
my hair is still and lank.
I see you shiver, blue-fingered:
fires pound and roar along my veins.
a thousand spectres dance and jerk
in your gaze, plucking your sleeve,
but I am swamped in white fog, light-blind
while you shudder in darkness.

no two people ever stand on the same side of a grave.

but if you fall across the chasm
toward me, and I fall toward you,
our hands may clasp in the middle
and make bridge of our bodies,
and your palms and mine will share the same heat.

magpies and majors

the magpies and I are at war.

petty skirmishes, really, but we draw close
in conflict, learning each other
as friends do not, this intimacy
born of angst one I do not want
to lose,
even as I defend my finches and nuthatches.

I wonder about soldiers,
if they do not feel more bound,
more brothered,
with their adversaries
than with the pretty painted finches
who sit at home,
waiting hungrily for safe, soft bread.

Carpenter on the Paris Train

I watched her on a late train
in Paris – he came coaxing at her threshold,
whispering slow dark words against her skin
till she built a room of her hair
and drew him in, shutting the night
fast outside the reach of their mingled breaths:

she painted her lintels with his oaths,
wordless avowals of eternity equally satisfied
by the swift eternity of an instant
if only her mouth is here, her crafter's fingers
framing his face, framing all the world
he will ever want or wants right now:

I am envious of this carpenter
and her stick-built house: all the storms
of Paris cannot rob her of this hour,
this space, this kiss,
she has built in the room of her hair.

Violin Vigil for Elijah McClain

she began to play at five:
a long, tedious affair bereft
of pleasures. unlike lovers more
easily wooed, the violin holds
her secret self in abeyance
till long after the shoulders are sore,
the fingers calloused, the ears ringing:
years pass before she begins to yield,
to trade sweet kisses for earnest caresses,
and still she will not tell
all her stories:

but today, today, my girl
and her violin do not sing for themselves

today, they sing for Elijah

Elijah, whose story has been spilled
like blood, whose secrets were torn
like broken strings, whose shattered body
like shattered wood lies at the foot
of our nation's pyre
and begs incendiency:

song rises aflame with fury,
but this melody does not belong to him

his notes are silence and smoke.

they called her a vegetable

in the ocean, the line between flora
and fauna is forever being scrubbed away
with sand and salt: the long tresses
of mermaids drowned in the sun litter
the shores like seaweed, petals plucked
from the sea floor peer with pensive faces
from the waves, and even stones sing:

perhaps, then, our nomination is mistaken,
our delineation too narrow,
and this sheeted, intubated soul is less vegetable
and more sea jelly, not stunted and still
in dark unyielding earth
but adrift on tides we cannot feel,
bound for shores we cannot see.

a hard life's work

light pools in a leaf
above my head, but I do not fear
its fall: not fire but golden oil
spills onto my hair,
fills my palms

I am not mistress but well-missed
and as a bought beloved,
I must pay for my patronage
with calloused hands and bloodied heels –

I fear the thorns
but still hope to wear them

dread the nails
but long for the taste of iron

if it means you too are anointed
with me: every keeper of slaves
is kept by slavery

every bearer of hatreds
is borne to the same hated grave,
but we two, if we will share the lash,
may break it in the end:

feed me honey
I have brought you a pitcher of milk
let all the leaves fall.

some animals

congresses and murders and packs
and schools become symphonies
outside these walls – weeds gallop
out of the snow and shake off the weak grip
of lawns and gardens, the trees hold hands
across overgrown trails and build canopies
beneath skies gone blue again:

we watch from our cages
as our poor scribbles are erased
from the canvas and the old oils rubbed clean,
and we swear, we swear,

we will honor the ancient frame,
we will stain our fingers and feet
with these heirloom paints,
but all the while our bellies growl
for plastic meat, and we bite our nails,
rattle the bars, bend the locks,
eager, eager,
to rush back upon the green till it is black again.

solitary confinement

I am building a folly on the edge
of the sea: walls of quartz and coal,
steps of driftwood, windows framed
with fishbones and chiton shells,
sea-gusts for mortar and a roof of clouds:

I will climb my tower and look
for you, and over the mountains – I hope
you are building a folly too,
hope your hands are dusty and calloused,
your eyes crusted with sand
and your feet bare on the cliffside path:

send up a signal
in the smoke of the cathedrals,
and I will say your name loud
in my empty halls,
I will trace in bruises
the echo of your voice on my chest.

Our Mother's Children

I have forgotten their names,
she is muttering, her arms clasped
'round her knees as she rocks herself
back and forth, and I must
lean in, strain to hear her
over the planes and the shouting
and the crumbling,
but I am grateful to pretend
this is more important, that her words
carry more weight than those bombs do –

whose names, I ask,
and her eyes clutch mine,
full of tears.
My children's names, she says,
but she has no children.

likely neither of us
will ever have children,
likely neither of us
have more than a month, a week,
an hour of our own,
but now I too am crying,
rocking myself in empty arms like a babe:

we have all lost,
we have all forgotten
the names of our children,
of our mother's children,
we heap graves upon them
we cannot mark.

belay that order

ghost-boats bob beneath the waves,
caught in tides our moon no longer
measures: no noble galleons,
with proud prows and graceful sterns,
these drifting tombs hardly pretended
to be sea-worthy even as they lured
oil-faced spectres who used to be
men and boys, women and girls and babies,
to flee the shores and turn instead for refuge
to these flotilla of rubber and patches and air:

they drift like seaweed
they cling to the barnacles
building up on the bottom of our boats

I watch the water rise
as we sink
becoming ghost-nations buried in our own sea.

Paris and her fripperies

an old sofa, sodden with rain
and fog and filth, shivers in the shadow
of a huge stone arch on a Paris street,
its cushions stuffed with trash,
and beneath the austere gaze of a stone lion,
an array of concert stickers and half-hearted graffiti
proclaims nothing comprehensible

gargoyles vie with clutches of leather-clad
smokers and scarf-draped men in fancy shoes,
broad-shouldered tenements hunch obstinate
beside ancient pillars and scream spray-painted
protests at the trains hurtling by
(though the travelers inside are all dozing
or lost in the thrall of their phones,)
and hosts and hostesses hawk menus
to passing tourists while an old cathedral
looks on with smoke-singed eyes:

I wonder who best protects
these streets and stories, whether the city
bides in the catacombs or in the purse shops,
in stained glass and bronze eyes
or in political posters and piles of rags,
and I decide, inhuman as I surely am,
I will take the gargoyles' part,
I will stand observer, look past
the fripperies of flesh and time
and keep my eyes on what is real and unseen.

only fools would

we will not save them, of course

their blood is on their own heads
they chose to leave the land
they chose to take to sea
in an inflatable rubber boat
(ninety-one, this time, but there are
so many times) they chose
to drown the same way I have seen
men choose to fall, to plunge
hundreds of feet and dash their brains out
on concrete sidewalks to escape an inferno

so we will neither save them
from the waves or put out the fire
at their backs: this is all
their own fault, their own choice,
and even the merest sympathy is swallowed up
with resentment we should be made to feel at all.

what's that name

behind me, a white girl –
I'm not white, she assures me,
I'm white-passing –
cheerily shouts the wrong name
as she wields her megaphone
with the authority of a soccer mom
at a PTA meeting
or a middle-school cheerleader,
and I rush to correct her.

Let it go, someone says,
that's not the point,
and I wonder, then what's the point?

we've but barely seized
on these snuffed souls,
championed them only in their absence –
so much more comfortable that way –

and now, like often,
like always, like Ellis,
we misspeak their names
to fit our own tongues,
we rewrite their characters
to make them more worthy
of the justice we keep hoarded in our pockets,
we repaint their colors
and our own to make a pretty picture.

Syrian grandmother

there is a body lying in the corner
of the tent, a body still alive
in all the ways we measure animus

air proceeds in and out of the lungs
with a terrible regularity,
the heart trudges on as if it will never stop,
eyelids water the orbs that have long since
ceased their weeping,
but still, it is only a body

the soul, a mother's soul, is out wandering

her son believes it is because
his brother is dead, erased in prison,
but it is because she has learned
they are all dead

she used to be like her son,
used to be desperate and determined
to save her babies, save them all,
but today, as cold rattles the tent walls
and the booming sounds
two hills away
one hill away

she only hopes she is wandering
and not awake when the booming strikes
this hill, and her last son
and his three daughters aren't desperate anymore.

practicing scales

my rhythm sticks and swings
with the arm of the metronome
that strikes on concrete dust crumbling
in Wisconsin and on burnt kangaroos
crawling in Australia and on bone cancer
praying in a pew at church
and somewhere between the beats
I draw the bow
across my own guts
and find resonance with the voice
of the sea ice strangling the bay.

A Child, My Child, in India

water

reflecting sky,
reflecting the faces
of his parents, angry

reflecting leaves
and branches
and tires stopped on an empty road

he always loved water

but he couldn't breathe in it

couldn't find the sky
when his parents were clouds
and the alligators came

and he was just trash
in the river:

voiceless,

the bones that were left,
when the alligator was full,
and his parents' car was empty.

Dires of Palestine

bigger than a wolf,
the beast pads through broken streets
and lopes the new geography
of crumbled mosques, cemetery houses,
and hills of bone and shattered stone,
his brimstone breath slavering
over teeth black as burned olive trees,
but the dull eyes that follow after him
see only a gust of smoke,
perhaps rubble dust,
borne along by breezes and despair:

always hungry and never filled,
he and his brothers rise from the cracked earth,
the cracked bricks, and the cracked fingers
of mothers and fathers who claw
their lifeless children from the grasp
of bombs and missiles and bullets,
and night and day they hunt –

tracing tiny bloody footprints
through flour discarded on the streets,
and following the tear tracks
of grandfathers on stones that cannot be lifted,
they make meal after meal of misery,
but every dawn
they must glut themselves anew.

détente

selkies and sand-fairies have long been at war

I know this,
not from storybooks or songs,
but from the hollow place
in my belly where babies once slept:

it is the same sort of battle
that sends starlight surging
across galaxies, straining
to glimmer on the lost faces of pallasites,
a blow that aches like a caress

so I play mediator

sifting the black sand
for even the tiniest of unshattered spiral shells,
leaving them as offerings
on stones stained by high tide marks

and when I squint into the light,
where the sun wicks fog from the waves
and sends it billowing and tumbling
over the shore, I stand signatory
as the seal-folk shed their skins,
and the sand-fairies fold away
their abrading wings to trade treasures
with their former families
and – no doubt – hatch common plots
against us mortal grabbers
with our open mouths and clenched fists and dirty,
dirty, oil-stained feet.

**influenza is callous,
or callousness is a fever that kills**

she will cry when the grape pops
in her mouth, and the grief will be a surprise,
a reprisal for what might have been
joy or delight or even only pleasure,
only thirst slaked sweet

the last time she tasted grapes,
her baby girl was still just a baby

still alive

before the long, hard, dirty road
of thousands of miles –
all those multitudes of fears,
all those agonies and aches,
all that intention,
swallowed up and consumed
in a few hours of fever
in a cage on the "safe" side of a border

she will cry one day, months or years
from now, when the grape pops
in her mouth, and she remembers
cutting fruit into little pieces,
and how her daughter's tiny face
pursed and scowled at the sour-sweet taste

but for now, there are no days,
no months, no years,
no flavors,
only the grit of dust in her eyes
and in her teeth
and in an empty baby blanket.

Platsdarm

chroniclers and archivists and death-song singers:
like soldiers they tramp boggy battlefields
and ghost through muddy trenches,
like priests they collect scattered rosary beads
and lift fallen crosses,
like hunters they reconstruct sagas and calamities
from boot prints and ball caps and bones

dollmakers and detectives,
with dry eyes and raw fingers and plastic bags,
they gather all the pieces
to put other mothers' and fathers'
sons and daughters back together

cracks radiate like starlight
from the hole in a helmet
where a soul slipped out

they dig broken teeth out of the ground
and mail a story's ending home
in a padded envelope, whose stamps
promise a further destination
than the post can reach.

Palm Sunday

bodies fall in the streets
like palm leaves cast down
by onlookers huddled safely –
they think –
out of reach of the trampling hooves

no king leads this procession,
only a cannibal,
the gluttonous folds of his belly
securing his seat
on the blindfolded ass waddling
its way down the cobblestones

hosanna, whisper the bystanders,
their alleluias hardly heard
over the jingle of coins in their pockets

but their god is not among them,
or above them:
blood-spattered and mud-spattered,
hems rank with offal,
the Divine crawls among the fallen,
weeping like Rachel for her children.

cemetery songs

she sits in the back
of what passes for a makeshift ambulance,
catching sunlight and hand grenades
in her teeth
and spitting both out behind her
in the hard-baked ruts
of what were muddy roads

over and over,
she tells the same lie
to dying men,
to pieces of men,
to dead men
whose eyes haven't closed yet,
to men headed home
where no home remains

I got you – you're going to be okay

but for herself,
she needs no lies

she dug her own grave
before she left home

she keeps as sole comfort
the color of her wife's eyes
shadowed by sheets,
the glide of a heron's wings

over a still morning pond,
the fragrance of lilacs
crushed by summer storms

and with such solace,
she feels no fear.

cousins

cool rusted steel under our palms,
the sag of the gate as we clamber over,
all anxious giggles and choking breaths
while we keep weather-eyes out on the grazing cows
we are sure will become rampaging bulls
at any moment – we sidestep stickers
and garter snakes and strike out for shade,
setting up our secret camp
in a dried-out creekbed under a tangle
of cottonwoods and crabapples –
we collect cicada shells and talk about Stephen King
novels
and real-life ghosts and stray cats

and years later, when we haven't seen each other
since the last funeral
and we have nothing left in common
but the intersections of our mutual failures –
failed marriages and lost jobs and lost children –
we can squint against a muggy Oklahoma sun
to peer into each other's eyes
and see there dragonflies and Arkansas diamonds
and little piles of red dirt heaped on the graves
of kittens behind the barn,
and somehow,
we still belong to each other.

keepers

yellow nicotine and brown dirt
etch a tattoo deeper than ink
on a man's fingers –
they shake when he rolls cigarette paper,
but hold steady as stone
when he grips his gun

a woman comes home,
emptied of her purpose,
emptied of her organs,
a teller of truths
whose body could not be forced
to speak a lie

a dog with muddy paws
sleeps beside a marble door
that only opens one way.

A Man and His Mother and a Rabbit

Easter week at the soup kitchen:
I wonder where he got it,
a bright white bunny with pink stitches,
its velvet nose untroubled
by the evening's miasma of marijuana,
old smoke, body odor,
and teriyaki chicken

it watches with unscuffed eyes
as he deftly deals cards
between his mother and himself,
UNO their game of choice:
only coffee for us tonight,
he tells me,
today's payday,
so he's taking her out to a real restaurant

but for now,
they and the rabbit he got her
find comfort in old metal chairs
and a plastic table,
their banter its own note
amid the symphony of friends
and strangers finding fellowship
in a place that offers safety
for an hour and a half

I won! he crows,
his eyes outshining the rabbit's.
I never win.
I won tonight.

Visdeurbel: 493 Watching

there are 493 of us tonight:
at least, it's night here,
the brightest stars shouting their names
over the babble of streetlights
and headlights and blazing windows,
while owls and mice and raccoons
and coyotes conduct their business
in the midnight twilight of suburbia

493 of us – taken alongside the billions
of people breathing,
that number feels intimate,
and I wonder at this net that binds
us each to the other,
knotted at our computer screens
and at a camera in a canal in Utrecht,
watching water bugs flit by
as sunlight I cannot feel
filters through the currents of a river
on whose banks I have never walked,
and together, we 493,
wait to ring a doorbell
and save a fish

this net, I think,
is fashioned of more threads
than the one that begins
and ends in the Netherlands:
we must love each other,
we 493:
what else will we do,
what else might we catch in our net?

afternoon at the river

she steps from the water
more wind than woman,
river silt between her toes
and dragonfly song tangled in her hair

on her tongue,
she tastes the mountain peaks,
and the fragrances of pine and fir
intoxicate each inhalation

translate each exhalation
into a language shared
with roots and stones and flowers
and spores

she walks a dusty path
under the regard of a warm spring sun,
her wet skirts clinging
to her calves, her thighs

and she is sad,
so sad,
when they dry.

Class Assignment

it is not unique to tyrants –
at least,
it is not unique to those tyrants,
to ask children to carry
the weight of war
in their small backpacks and small hearts

to put ink and grief and guilt
and construction paper
into their hands
and demand they tell strangers with guns:
thank you for killing other strangers -
maybe with guns, maybe not

to illustrate love and fear
with stick figures and circle suns
and trees whose bright fruit
will all rot ungathered on the ground

perhaps it is unique to tyrants,
perhaps we are all tyrants,
eating at tables set by grandmothers
our sons have killed.

Belly of Grass

green and blue the waves, so bright
        the light as I lay drowning,
the sea that stole the rigor from my bones
        and held the breath fast in my throat
no sea of salt but only grass, endless
        grass, seething sunrise to sunset,
relentless tides of prairie carrying me nowhere,
        motion, motion, but no movement:

my eyes were bleached sightless with light,
        and no shore relieved my aching gaze,
the sky held me down below the surface,
        willed my flesh to become the earth
as those grasses grew through my belly –
        I ripped them out.

uprooted, excised, evulsed: I tore them
        from me, slipped the moorings
anchoring my limbs to this sullen sea,
        and embarked on the wind instead:
my belly is full of holes, reminders
        of my recent thrall and its treachery.
but I thrust my fingers into the stigmata
        and find the promise of breath beyond the waves.

the golden mole: a mystery

a sun hidden in the earth,
star of rainbows
whose mirror lies deep in the sea,
where bioluminescence is the name
modern folk give ancient magic

on blue sky days,
ocean breaths bubble up,
frothing iridescent on the shore
and making gems of broken pebbles

while trundling away underground,
unseen, unsung, unguessed-at,
that hidden sun burrows its merry tunnels,
gleaming, glowing, a-glitter,
and we think it ignorant
of its own singular glory,
we think its strange beauty unremarked
by any other being

but what do we know of universes,
after all,
we who imagine the nearest sister
to our star must be light-years away,
and cannot be beneath our skin,
beneath the thin-stretched skin of the earth?

When It All Began

We are documenting everything, they said

I picture desktop files labeled
dead children
dead grandmothers
dead uncles
dead goldfish

we will trace in faint grayscale lines
old boundaries – how will we draw
the bridges that now lie in rubble?

we can make lists of suitcase contents
spilled on the streets,
number bones by their hours:
>   these are afternoon corpses
>   these are evening corpses
>   these are morning corpses

scientists can measure saline in the soil
we will send in a mother with garbage bags
to bring us back all the empty shoes

people in uniforms with chests full of old bravery
will stare at screens,
watching and nodding as shells scream by

We are documenting everything, they say.

family traditions

I will be scarred
like the earth is scarred,
I will not hide my wounds

I will burl my broken limbs

where time cuts its grooves
deep into my flesh,
I will bring forth rivers.

salt what was fertile,
and I will call upon mallow,
on samphire and saltbush and limonium

pock me with holes,
and seas will rise to fill them

I will look on the end
with the eyes of an octopus

and in a sky-burial,
I will welcome what feeds
and carries my cells to the currents.

Paint-By-Numbers World

we paint each other by numbers,
counting out worth *one, two, three*:

it's the third world, after all –
they don't get hungry like we do –
they're used to rice.

it's good for them.

see how happy they look on their bicycles?

the sun is good for them.

we should learn from them, they're so content.

they have fantastic immune systems,
those third world people.

it's hard to watch them always killing
each other, but they're not like us,
are they?

are they?

are they like us?

are we only one number away

from hunger, from thirst, from disease,
from killing each other in the streets
with clubs?

or are we already counted,
one, two, three,
already hungry, already sick, already wounded

all dressed up for the grave
in Big Mac wrappers and Nike shoes.

Acknowledgments

some animals and *solitary confinement* first published
December 2020 by Alternative Field in their chapbook
In Isolation

song for the unfound and *a hard life's work* first
published December 2020 by Poetry South

Our Mother's Children and *revolt* first published
September 2022 in Setu Magazine's Freedom Issue

Syrian grandmother first published October 2022 in
the IHRAF Anthology *A Human Voice*

Dires of Palestine first published Winter 2024 in the
HWA Poetry Showcase, Volume XI

THE AUTHOR

In addition to ten novels, **Cassondra Windwalker** is the poet of three previous poetry collections: *The Almost-Children, The Bench,* and *tide tables and tea with god. The Bench* was awarded the 2020 Helen Kay Chapbook Award by Evening Street Press. *tide tables and tea with god* earned the Excellence in Poetry Award from Cinnabar Moth Press in 2022, and she served as their poet-in-residence in 2023. Her poems have also been included in numerous literary journals and anthologies. She presently writes from the Front Range of Colorado Rocky Mountains.